Foreword

What you're about to read might sound like a spiritual sci-fi; it transcribes the broadcast of a human passenger of MotherShip Terra - our planet in the shifting paradigm from humankind to kind human to steward of this world.

A lot of signs - coming through dreams and synchronicities - encouraged, supported, and guided me to write this book. It was a very intense process, and at its end I cried with joy feeling a profound emotion very similar to the one when I got to hold each of my children for the first time.

I am a native Romanian; however, thinking and writing this directly into English came naturally, like it was meant to be, a gift from above. Each text was carefully crafted. Each idea, with each word used for it, was played until my heart echoed the voice in my mind. This work turned out to be rather channeling; it would sometimes leave me dizzy and in awe, make me stop and exclaim "What?!!!" with tears in my eyes.

Imagine a box with a mix of let's say 5000 pieces from different puzzles, all beautiful, all different, all fascinating. You're told that you need to find the 21 pieces that fit together to display a certain image and that you have to figure it out for yourself. That's how my twenty-one texts arrived and were assembled to convey the picture of our journey(s) on Earth and with the Earth; I used the name Terra for our planet (the Latin word for Earth) to avoid confusion between planet Earth and the Earth element and the word Terrans for all of its life forms. During this process, some new words were born, that you will not find in any dictionary but are easy to understand. I also aimed for simplicity and clarity, a message for all.

Thank you for allowing me to share my broadcast with you as an act of Love.

Nicoleta Taylor

TERRANS

Nicoleta Taylor

To MotherShip Terra's Stewards, with Love

Paperback ISBN: 978-953806-96-3
Ingram Spark Paperback ISBN: 978-1-958405-00-0
Ebook ISBN: 978-1-953806-97-0
Library of Congress Control Number: 2022905830

Interior Design: Amit Dey

http://www.amazon.com/author/nicoletataylor

Table of Contents

Foreword 3

Acknowledgments. 7

Prologue. 13

S.O.S. 15

Genesis. 17

One Country 19

Guidance 21

Fire 27

Air. 29

Water 31

Earth. 35

Love 37

Blueprint 41

Odyssey 47

Affirmation. 49

Materialization 51

Broadcast 53

Contact. 55

Other 61

Home 63

Legacy. 65

Epilogue. 69

Just Kidding 71

Gratitude 75

About the Author 79

Acknowledgments

It has been a joy getting to know Nicoleta Taylor. We met while serving as contributing authors of chapters to a collaborative book about wisdom and grace. Nicoleta embodies both of these lovely qualities in abundance. After reading her story about being a traveler here on earth, her gifted imagination quickly became evident. However, I soon learned that her talent far exceeds just putting words on paper. Her writing is truly heartfelt, but it also causes the reader to think deeply about the imagery being expressed.

This is a pivotal time in human history. People are waking up as if from a long sleep. Every living form on Terra is connected and we truly are ONE. I encourage you, the reader, to share this book of inspired poems. As we support each other in rising to higher energy frequency vibrations, those energies will ripple out in the most beautiful and unexpected ways. This is a book about hope.

Norma-Jean Strickland
Positive change activist in support of conscious evolution
Published author and editor
Classical musician and educator
Idea generator
www.linkedin.com/in/normajeanstrickland

To know Nicoleta is to know goodness and sparkle. Nicoleta Taylor brings fresh perspective and food for thought in the beautiful work she offers the world in the pages of this book. Nicoleta's light shines bright in a world that can be very confusing and frightening at the same time.

She reminds us of how interconnected we truly are, and how important it is to value our connections with both the seen and unseen. Truly our world and the universes beyond are filled with vibrational frequencies that support us on our life's journey.

Nicoleta's amazing collection of poetry in this book will reignite the knowingness that we are never alone and that our thoughts and actions do have a vibrational ripple effect that reaches a never-ending universe that is our world.

Becky Norwood
Book Publishing Expert/CEO Spotlight Publishing
https://spotlightpublishing.pro

Prologue

The scale from
void
to
infinity,
where void embeds
the unmanifested potential
and infinity unfolds
the progressive manifestation
of the Source,
chronicles
our journey
within the Source.

Bodies,
starlight to stardust.
Spirits,
starlight to life.

Quo Vadis, Terrans?

S.O.S.

Eons ago
ten riches of the old universe
were embodied
on the ten live planet ships
of the Sun fleet,
aided by
live moon satellites,
navigating the waves
of the new universe,
destination
the Source headquarters.

This is Terra,
the third ship flanking
the Sun, our Star FatherShip,
gravity and energy embedded.

Terra is the ark,
the MotherShip,
and her cargo
is Life.

Along this voyage
her blueprint was bypassed
and now the stewards
misuse her
as disposable resource.

This exploitation is causing
Life-threatening damage.
It has escalated to
dangerously low levels of Love
causing disturbances
of the Fire, Water, Air,
and Earth elements.
Half of Life,
with its billions of passengers,
is already extinct.

Sending out an S.O.S.
M.S. Terra is now leaking
the Love element.

Genesis

Once upon a time
in the land of the green,
the mighty Panther King
was wishing for a Queen.

He asked the tender Bird,
his dear soul mate,
to join him on the throne,
become his Queen, his fate.

They took the human shape
when all the stars aligned,
worshipped through Terran day,
invoked through Terran night.

Their Love was Water,
their Love was Fire,
their Love brought to the world
 the true Life desire.

Their Love was Air,
their Love was Earth,
Their Love brought to the world
the true Life rebirth.

Twelve noble Children
were born of their kind
to travel through millennia
as teachers of mankind.

Six Queenlike Daughters
and six Kinglike Sons
to bear many mighty names
and still be called the Ones.

Since upon that time
in the land of the green,
the world's been ruled with Love
by the G(o)od King
and his Queen.

One Country

I live in a Country called Terra
neighboring Mars and Venus
in the realm of the Sun.

My species is Human
and we speak Human.
It's the language we mostly use
for now
although here and there
there are Humans
who speak God,
like all of our kin,
animate and inanimate beings.

At birth,
we receive the Terran residence,
and after death

we can travel to other realms,
although, here and there,
there are Humans
able to travel
under the current restrictions.

My faith is in the One,
and my religion is Love,
although (s)he, the One,
is still called by different names
in various parts of Our Country.
For now.

Our Country has Water and Fire,
and Air and Earth,
conjoined by Love.
Ah, the breathtaking landscape
and the myriads of Life forms
that they shape and nurture.

Our Country is so beautiful.
Stranger, where are you from?

Guidance

Upon arrival to MotherShip Terra
remember that
she is alive.
Living matter births living matter.
The Earth, Water, Air, and Fire
of your spacesuit,
are of her.
She is intelligent,
evolving,
enabling your Spirit
to fully experience
its Terran journey.
Remember that your Spirit
loves and honors her Spirit,
siblings from the same Source.
There is more Life,
more travelers in their spacesuits

than your senses can detect
and your mind can define:
a living oneness.
Remember that your Spirit
loves and honors their Spirits,
younger and older,
siblings from the same Source.

Some equipment
of their spacesuits
 has been impacted
by the collision with the Other.
Yours might get exposed too.
Remember that you are more
than your spacesuits.
Remember that your Spirits
are still intact inside
and recognize each other.
Light
is the fastest agent in the universe.
Darkness is only its absence.
In an instant
it is up to your free will
to illuminate your course,

heal yourself
and start healing
the Other.

Your Earth, Water, Air, and Fire
have long been here
before you came,
will long be here after you leave.
You're not bringing anything with you
other than Love,
you will not be taking anything back
other than Love,
you will not be leaving anything behind
other than Love.

You are a steward
of M.S. Terra.
Live with her
respecting all Life.
Leave her
suitable for all Life.

Enlighten your thoughts.
What would Love say?
What would Love do?

Catalyze your actions.
Say what Love would say.
Do what Love would do.

Authenticate their manifestation.
It is what Love says,
It is what Love does.

Good
Om
Deus.

Fire

Source.
Singularity evolving,
expanding,
beaming
primordial light.
Sourcestarlight.

Wave-particle oneness of
Sourcestarlight energy
dancing through the universe,
synchronizing stardust
and portraying matter.

Fire element,
Sourcestarlight plasma,
fueling
FatherShip Sun,

its gravity
the Sun Fleet's core,
its brilliance
the Sun Fleet's illumination
and beacon of Life.

Fire element,
fueling
the cells
of your spacesuit,
firing your neurons,
purifying your Self,
enlightening your Terran journey.

You are a steward of MotherShip Terra.
How Life forging is your Fire?
How bright is your Light?

Air

The breath of the Source,
starlight
transmuted into
stardust.

Air element,
the dome of gases
shielding MotherShip Terra,
the breathable stardust
of your spacesuit,
is her air,
the placenta of Life,
if unaltered
by unnatural processes.

Living wind
inhaled
and exhaled,
flowing in,
out,
and around
every spacesuit,
blowing
Life sustenance,
airmailing
information.

Sound medium,
your voice,
your body's backing vocals,
M.S. Terra's fragrant music.

Collective field
blanketing the world
with oneness.

You are MotherShip Terra's steward.
Do you take her Air for granted?
Does your Heart beat
and your Voice speak
for all Life?

Water

Hydrogen,
Sourcestarlight's
most abundant matter embodiment
in the universe.
Oxygen,
Sourcestarlight's
most abundant matter embodiment
on MotherShip Terra.
Water element,
their intelligent union,
liquid stardust,
the amniotic fluid of Life.

Water,
mothering myriads of life forms,
spirits inhabiting
their custom equipment
for the Terran experience.

Water,
entering your body,
becoming your water,
the fluid filling your spacesuit,
your Life solvent,
your sustenance,
your cleanser,
flowing through your body,
leaving your body
as your mist,
your dew,
your rain,
in perpetual exchange and interaction
with all water,
has flowed
through all Terran passengers,
learning.

If unaltered
by unnatural processes
Water is alive,
intelligent,
remembers,
streams
evolutionary information exchange
between Life forms.

You are MotherShip Terra's steward.
Your body is a Water grail.
How pure have you been upkeeping
your refilling Life fountain?

Earth

Sourcestarlight's shape,
solid stardust.

Earth element,
the corps of the solid building blocks
perfectly assembling
Life geometric encoded spacesuits.

Oneness of elemental entities,
108 coexisting in formations
suitable for Terran Life.

Recyclable materials that
if unaltered
by unnatural processes

sustain the cycle of building
and maintaining
Terra-dimensional living spacesuits.

Ah, the myriads of inanimate
and animate spacesuits,
standing,
floating,
crawling,
hopping,
walking,
flying,
swimming
in symbiosis
and continuous
substance exchange
with our MotherShip Terra
herself,
then reintegrating
with her,
matter for
future Life.

The end of a spacesuit's usability cycle
is commonly known as Death.

Love

Let me hold you.
You've never been alone.

Your birthing takes
the oneness of
Fire, Air, Water, and Earth
with Love
to become Life.

This gravity
keeping your atoms and electrons
in perfect alignment,
the space between them,
keeping Sun and Terra,

Terra and Moon
in perfect harmony,
the space between them,
is Love.

Love,
the archelement,
designing and manifesting
the sublime beauty
of the universe.

This free-will gravity,
drawing us together
and keeping us close
regardless of the space
and worlds between us,
is Love.

Everyone and everything
touching your soul
and brightening your light
is Love.
Human and non-human family,
friends, strangers,
Terra's breathtaking beauty,
all works of Life art and engineering,

co-existing,
if unnaturally unaltered,
the splendor of the night sky,
the brilliance of the sunshine,
all Love artistry.

The greatest treasure
is in plain sight.

You are Love.
The creation element,
the designer and weaver of Life
is in you,
IS you.

This Source energy
carrying our creator's
information -
shape,
emotion,
intelligence,
compassion,
program,
oneness,
potential -
is Love.

Love is the miracle
of your moving, feeling, thinking,
breathing, sensing spacesuit.
Love is the wonder
of your ideas, imagination,
dreams, visions inside it.
You are a Love phenomenon.

Love element,
known as quintessence,
the fifth element,
actually prime-essence,
the first element,
spirit above matter.
Your spirit,
child of the Source,
inheriting its potential.
Love is all there is.

Let me hold you.
You've never been alone.

Blueprint

Infinity-D Source
manifesting as
Spirit
substantiating as
Spacesuit
itSelfing as
Terra-D Human.

Earth element.
Red.
0-8
Body:
Life navigation DNA-designed spacesuit.

Water element.
Orange.
8-13

Emofeeling:
Self-perception compass,
Life navigation sensor.

Fire element.
Yellow.
13-21
Mind:
Self-configuration control panel,
Thought transmitter,
Life navigation processor.

Air element.
Green.
21-34
Heart:
Self-field generator,
collective field antenna,
relationship radar,
Life navigation engine.

Love element.
Blue.
34-55
Soul:

Self-expression materializer,
free will sound system,
communication software,
relationship synchronizer,
Life navigation program.

Love element.
Indigo.
55-89
Third eye:
Self-vision lens,
sixth sense camera,
Source channel,
multiverse travel portal,
past-lives projector,
Life navigation light.

Love element.
Violet.
89-...
Spirit:
Self-consciousness,
Source quintessence,
Source energy,
Source oneness component,

spacesuit builder,
spacesuit power source,
Life navigation pilot.

All elements
o-...
White.
Whole Human.

Om.
Aum.
I Am.

Odyssey

Life is the arch of a rainbow.
Ephemeral mystery,
suspended between
the earth and the sky,
fed by the sun and the rain,
and by the Love quintessence
within us.

When at the divine space agency
we received the blessing for
the Terran destination,
to fully be here, we signed
that we agree to blur
our previous journeys.
We were each given
a human body vehicle,
complexly programmed

for the terrestrial environment,
recyclable on departure,
material for future generations.

Life is the arch of a rainbow.
Perfectly incomplete,
from red searching for its red
to purple for its purple,
each color
looking for itself
and meeting with itself
in a given time
and space.

And when they find each other,
and merge into each other,
Death is the round rainbow,
the perfectly full circle,
portal to other worlds,
to the divine Source,
our first family,
home,
and resource.

Affirmation

Our Source Father-Mother,
sacred is your name.

Your Love conceives.

Your Essence manifests
on Terra
as in all your Creation.

You give us
here
our Air, Water,
Earth, Fire, and Love
Life sustenance.

You forgive us
when we don't say

what Love would say
and don't do
what Love would do
as we forgive
ourselves
and we forgive
those
who don't say to us
what Love would say
and don't do to us
what Love would do.

Enlighten our choices
and set us free
from what is not of you:
For yours is our everything,
now
and forever.

Materialization

At first, it was
a thought of Love
whispered in the Light
traveling the universe
to and through
the smile of the Source
and back where,
woven within
Water,
and Fire,
and Air,
and Earth,
it became you,
my sweet child.

Broadcast

Sweet child,
this is MotherShip Terra speaking.

We're both alive.
Your spirit is my sibling,
lights lifeforged
in our Sourcestarlight's Fire.
Your body is my child,
spacesuit life-built
with my Earth, Water, and Air.

I, you, and my myriads of passengers
are evolving together.
(Re)embarking on this Terran voyage
is your choice
to continue growing
as humankind
and more.

Kind human,
you are a steward
of Life.
Yours included.
Young humans
play mother and father.
Adult humans
act Source Father-Mother
when their Love
safeguards Life,
and safekeeps my Earth and Water,
Air and Fire,
the sustenance of all Life.

Sweet child,
when you think Love,
and speak Love,
and do Love,
you ascend co-creation.

Contact

You were there when
the toddler I,
lost on a frozen white winter night,
was "miraculously" found alive.

You were there when
the child I,
running in front of an unforgiving truck,
was "miraculously" one second faster.

You were there when
the teenager I,
targeted by a disturbed armed man,
was "miraculously" left unharmed.

You were there when
the adult I,
out of body after a deadly car crash,
was "miraculously" awakened unhurt.

You've always been
here and now
to
guide,
protect,
help,
inspire,
teach,
elevate,
awake
us.

Sometimes I would glimpse you:
a light,
an orb,
a shadow,
a shape in the clouds.

Sometimes I would sense you:
a touch,
a taste,

a scent,
a whisper,
an eye contact,
a smile,
a synchronicity.

Sometimes I would see some of you
and talk to you
in my vivid dreams.
I've called you many names
but your first names
are not of the Terran world.

You've always been here.
For me.
For all of your kin.

Contact acknowledged.

Other

You're not of my Source Father-Mother,
you're not of my world.

What is of you
in my world
is better left
unsensed,
unthought,
unsaid,
undone,
unmade,
unmanifested.

I wish you
Love.
To love
and
to be loved.

Fear
is not Love.
Power
is not Love.
Control
is not Love.

Only with Love
what is of you
will be
what you want it
to be.

Only then
the healing
will happen.

Home

When it was your time to leave,
mother,
you slipped out of your body
like out of your nightgown,
left it there, on the bed,
slightly wrinkled,
and then you stepped
into the light.

When it was your time to leave,
father,
you turned off your body,
a used vehicle
with the lifespan of one lifetime,
no warranty, no salvage,
and then you got out
 by the tunnel to heaven.

When it's my time to leave,
mother and father,
I will take off my body,
my cherished,
invaluable,
irreplaceable spacesuit
of Water and Fire,
and Air and Earth,
keeping only
the Love.

And then,
among the stars,
under your luminous guidance,
I will find my way
back home.

Legacy

I leave you my Love,
and take your Love with me,
our Love for each other
is the bridge across worlds
when we're physically apart.

Each generation worked
to build a better world,
but
absorbed into this process,
learning,
growing,
the big picture has blurred,
and
Love has not always been
the maker of our thoughts,

our words,
our actions.

We're getting there.

One day,
religion and science will merge,
dissolve into each other,
and become Love,
tapping directly into the Source.
That day,
if you believe
you know,
and
if you know
you believe.
Religion without Love
is faith at any cost,
science without Love
is knowledge at any cost,
for what is wisdom
if not
the alchemy of faith
and knowledge
into Love?

"As above - so below,
as below - so above.
As within - so without,
as without - so within.
As in great - so in small,
as in small - so in great."

Epilogue

This is
a human passenger
of the live Sun Fleet
at the moment 2021
of the eon of grace 4.543
since MotherShip Terra
was born
alive.

Over.

Just Kidding

How did Sourcestarlight dance
All You Need Is Love
(Across the Universe)?
Started burning: Fire.
Took a breath: Air.
Broke a sweat: Water.
Got some rest: Earth.

Gratitude

Thank you, *Florica* and *Niculaie Borz* – mom and dad in heaven, this book is the bridge of Love between our worlds.

This broadcast is my legacy for *Viktor*, *Peter*, and *Liliom Pataki* - my children and the greatest gifts of my life, and also for my great-niece *Silvia Torres*, my grandson *Julian Shafto*, and my unborn grandchildren, in the hope that it will help to shape a better world for all.

My gratitude goes to *Kevin Taylor* - my husband and hero without whom this book would have never been written.

A special thank you goes to *Adriana Borz* - my biological and soul sister, whose support motivated me to write this book and whose wise guidance helped me to refine it.

I also dedicate it to all of the amazing people below, in no particular order:

My niece *Anca Delgado*, for the special bond that turned us into sisters and her husband *César Torres* into my brother.

Andrea Pataki, Maggie Taylor, Analisa and *Justin Shafto*, the amazing adult children that life gifted me along this life journey.

My nephew *Adrian Heet*, who's always felt like a son, and his wife *Natascha*, my newly found daughter.

Ecaterina Borz - my second mother, and *Aurora* and *Constantin Niculae* - my second sister and brother.

Csaba Pataki, for our trials and tribulations.

My best friends forever *Nicoleta Paşca, Iulia Gavrilaş, Hajnal Egri, Anca Pop, Sherrie Buzby-Murasky,* and their families.

Paul Ştefan, for believing in me.

Orlando Balaş, whose environmental poetry inspired me.

All my *American, Romanian,* and *Hungarian* family and friends.

All my teachers, highlighting *Mrs. Viorica Borodi* and *Mrs. Ana Munteanu,* who instilled my love for reading and writing.

My *co-workers, business partners,* and *students,* for unexpected and inspiring friendships, and for teaching me Humanity.

My beautiful *Silver Sisters* - the co-authors of *Wisdom of the Silver Sisters* that hosts my first published story.

My *friends* all over the world.

All the *people* who crossed paths with me and touched my heart.

All the *people* whose work makes humankind better.

Freddie, our white German Shepherd, the non-human love of my life.

You, right now, when reading this.

My heartfelt thanks go to the special team that made this book a dream come true: *Becky*

Norwood – the outstanding publisher who said yes to it without hesitation, *Norma-Jean Strickland* for her most insightful proofreading work, *Sandy Rogers* and *Sharyn Jordan* for their most touching support and feedback, and *Florine Duffield* for taking the perfect portrait picture to match it.

And last but not least, my deepest gratitude goes to:

András Kovács-Magyar - spiritual master and the light upon my path, and his family.

My heavenly *guardians* and *helpers*.

Our home - *the Earth*, and our home's home – *the Solar System* and beyond.

The Elements that make this journey possible.

God - Our Source Father-Mother, for everything.

About the Author

Nicoleta Taylor was born in Transylvania, Romania, and moved to Phoenix, Arizona, in her forties. Her name reunites both her Romanian past and her American present.

While living in communist Romania, she found her refuge in books. In elementary school, she was already reading any novel that she could find during those hard times, imagining herself as a secret traveler witnessing other worlds. That was when she also started writing, mainly poems and fairytales. At the age of 14, she won *Someş Literary Presences* - a Transylvanian poetry contest, setting a record as the youngest poet ever to receive such an honor. At the age of 18, she was one of the top three finalists of the 1989 *Romanian Language and Literature National Contest*, which motivated her to pursue a B.A. in philology, majoring in Romanian and English.

After she became a mother of three children, her life challenges in Romania put her writing on hold. In 2010, she married her American soulmate and moved to Phoenix, Arizona, together with her children, where she rebuilt her life and started writing again. In 2011, she competed in the *"Text Construct" Romanian National Contest of Poetry and Short Prose*, where her short stories, *"The Last Bus"* and *"The Wheel of Fortune"* ranked her #3 nationwide. In 2021, she was invited to contribute to an American collective book, *"Wisdom of the Silver Sisters - Guiding Grace,"* a #1 Amazon international bestseller, recipient of the Firebird Award, and Barnes & Noble pick for the Biggest Books of the Fall.

While she continues writing poetry and prose, she has also authored courses and teaches Romanian language and culture for several language services providers with outstanding results and feedback from her American students. She collaborates with Ambrosius, a gifted team of dollmakers from Romania, by distributing their exquisitely handcrafted dolls in the U.S. market under the brand name *Eco Flower Fairies*. She is also doing work that makes her soul sing by helping those seeking a holistic spiritual approach to their issues, which earned her the Transylvanian Healer nickname.

You can learn more about her at:
http://www.amazon.com/author/nicoletataylor
www.linkedin.com/in/nicoleta-taylor-075a5410
www.ecoflowerfairies.com
www.transylvanianhealer.com

If you would like to reach out to her, she can be found at nicoleta.taylor@yahoo.com